Manifestation Demystified

The Real Science of Affirmations, Visualization, and Results

SHWETA JAISWAL

PUBLISHED BY: Shweta Jaiswal

Shweta Jaiswal

Dedication

To every seeker who ever wondered if manifestation is real — this book is for you.

Author's Note – Why I Wrote This Book

I wrote this book because I saw how much confusion exists around manifestation and affirmations. Some people blindly believe it's magic. Others reject it as fake. In reality, the truth lies in between.

Like many people, I also tried manifestation myself. I repeated affirmations, visualized, and waited for miracles — but nothing happened. I didn't succeed because I didn't understand the principles or how it truly works. My curiosity pushed me to dig deeper. I researched, studied, and experimented, only to discover that manifestation doesn't work the way most people think.

What I learned is simple: without action, nothing can happen. Thoughts and affirmations only set the stage — but the real change comes when your mind and actions align. That's when results begin to show up.

My goal with this book is to put together everything I discovered and present it in the simplest way possible. I've tried to break down the myths, show the science, and give you practical tools so you can see how manifestation actually works. Not just as a belief, but as a system based on psychology, neuroscience, and action.

This book is not about selling dreams. It's about giving you a reality check and a method you can rely on. If even one chapter helps you shift your mindset, take action, and change your life — this book has done its job.

— *Shweta Jaiswal*

Preface

Millions of people talk about manifestation and affirmations — some believe it's magic, others call it nonsense. But what's the truth?

This book is written to **burst the myths, explain the science, and give practical tools** so that anyone — student, professional, homemaker, or entrepreneur — can understand how manifestation really works.

No complicated language. No spiritual jargon. Only **simple explanations + real science + practical steps.**

By the end of this book, you will know exactly:

- What manifestation is (and isn't).
- The brain science behind affirmations and visualization.
- Common mistakes people make.

- A step-by-step blueprint that works in real life.
- Real case studies showing results.
- The **final truth**: fact or myth?

Table of Contents

PART 12 – Real-Life Case Studies & Experiments

PART 13 – Dangers, Misuse, and Toxic Positivity

PART 14 – Tools & Techniques That Actually Work

PART 18 – Busting Popular Myths About Manifestation

PART 19 – Building a Personal Manifestation System

PART 1

Introduction

Chapter 1 – What is Manifestation?

When people hear the word *manifestation*, they often imagine two extremes. Some think it's pure magic — that if you simply think hard enough about something, it will appear in your life.

Others laugh and dismiss it as nonsense — just another trend for people who want quick fixes.

👉 The reality is neither of those extremes.

Manifestation is not magic. But it is also not fake.

At its core, manifestation means:

The process of using your thoughts, focus, and beliefs to shape your actions, and through those actions, your reality.

The Brain as a Search Engine

Think of your brain as **Google.**
When you type "best pizza near me," Google shows millions of results for pizza. If you type "business books," you get completely different results.

Your thoughts work the same way. Whatever you focus on, your brain starts filtering the world to show more of it.

This happens because of something called the **RAS (Reticular Activating System)** in your brain.

- Example: If you're thinking of buying a red car, suddenly you start noticing red cars everywhere.
- The red cars were always there, but now your brain is filtering for them.

👉 This is one part of manifestation: when you focus your thoughts on a goal, your brain begins noticing opportunities that were invisible before.

Why People Confuse It with Magic

The misunderstanding comes from oversimplification.

- **Myth version:** "If I think about money, it will magically appear in my bank account."
- **Reality version:** "If I focus on financial growth, I'll notice chances to learn skills, earn, and save that I used to ignore."

One is wishful thinking.
The other is **focus → awareness → action → results.**

Example: Two Students Preparing for Exams

- **Student A**: Keeps repeating, "I'm going to fail anyway." Because of this belief, he avoids studying, misses opportunities to revise, and doesn't ask teachers for help.
- **Student B**: Repeats, "I can improve step by step." He notices useful notes, studies regularly, and asks questions in class.

Both students face the same exam.
But their **thoughts shaped their focus, which shaped their actions, which shaped their results.**

This is manifestation in real life.

Practical Exercise

Take a notebook and answer:

1. What is the biggest goal you have right now?
2. What thoughts do you normally think about it?
3. How do those thoughts influence your actions?

Notice the chain: **Thought → Focus → Action → Result.**

Summary

- Manifestation = thoughts shaping actions, not magic.
- Brain works like a search engine (RAS).
- Focus decides what you notice in the world.
- Beliefs → Focus → Actions → Results.

✦✦✦

Chapter 2 – History of Manifestation Beliefs

Manifestation is not new. People have believed in it in different forms for centuries.

Ancient Beliefs

- **Hinduism & Buddhism:** Karma and meditation taught that thoughts and intentions shape reality.
- **Stoic Philosophy (Greece/Rome):** Emphasized the power of the mind in creating inner peace and guiding action.
- **Christianity & Prayer:** Faith and words were seen as tools to invite divine guidance.

For thousands of years, humans believed that **thoughts had power.** Sometimes they linked it to gods, sometimes to energy, sometimes to the mind itself.

20th Century Popularity

In the early 1900s, a movement called **New Thought** became popular in the West. Books like *Think and Grow Rich* (Napoleon Hill, 1937) spread the idea that "thoughts become things."

Later, self-help gurus built on this, teaching people that affirmations and visualization could change life.

Modern Viral Trend

Today, manifestation exploded through social media platforms like YouTube, TikTok, and Instagram.

- People share vision boards, affirmations, and "success stories."
- The **Law of Attraction** became a buzzword: "Ask, Believe, Receive."

While some people genuinely benefit, others get stuck in magical thinking, expecting instant results without effort.

Why People Believe

Humans are naturally drawn to hope. We want to feel in control of our future. Manifestation gives us that feeling. Even if it's not magical, the belief itself can change how we act — and that can create real outcomes.

Summary

- Manifestation ideas existed in many ancient cultures.
- Modern self-help made it popular worldwide.
- Social media turned it into a trend.
- People believe because it gives hope and a sense of control.

✦✦✦

Chapter 3 – Modern Popularity: Why It Exploded

Why did manifestation become so popular in the last 20 years?

---

1. The Law of Attraction Movement

The book *The Secret* (2006) sold millions of copies worldwide. It promised that if you focus on positive thoughts, the universe will deliver your desires.

Though criticized by scientists, it gave people hope and an easy formula to follow.

---

2. Social Media Success Stories

On TikTok and YouTube, you'll find thousands of videos:

- People claiming they manifested jobs, relationships, money.
- Influencers showing "before and after" transformations.

These stories spread fast, even if they don't always show the hard work behind the scenes.

---

3. Stressful Times

When people face uncertainty (pandemics, financial struggles, personal problems), they naturally look for hope. Manifestation feels like a comforting tool.

---

4. The Appeal of Simplicity

Everyone wants a shortcut. Instead of years of effort, manifestation promises: *just think positive, and it will happen.*

That's why it spreads so quickly — it's easy to believe, even if not fully true.

Summary

- Books like *The Secret* boosted manifestation's fame.
- Social media created viral success stories.
- Stressful times made people seek hope.
- The idea of a shortcut attracted millions.

✦✦✦

Chapter 4 – Why People Believe It Works

If manifestation isn't magical, then why do so many people swear it worked for them?

---

1. Placebo Effect

When people believe something will work, their body and mind often respond positively. Just like a sugar pill can reduce pain if you believe it's medicine.

---

2. Focus & Action

When you repeat affirmations like "I will succeed," your brain filters for success opportunities. You act differently — more confident, more motivated.

---

3. Success Stories

Hearing others say "I manifested this" gives people hope. They connect the dots between their own effort and their belief, even if effort was the real driver.

---

4. Psychological Safety

Manifestation gives people a sense of control in an uncertain world. Even if outcomes are slow, the belief itself reduces stress and increases patience.

Summary

- Belief itself can create real effects (placebo).
- Focus changes actions and results.
- Stories of success spread the belief.
- Manifestation gives comfort in uncertainty.

✦✦✦

Chapter 5 – Our Goal in This Book

By now, you understand what manifestation is, where it came from, and why people believe in it.

But the real question is:
Is it **fact or myth?**

This book has one mission:

- To **burst the myths** around manifestation.
- To explain the **real science** behind affirmations, visualization, and belief.
- To give you a **practical blueprint** so you know exactly what works and what doesn't.

We won't sell dreams. We won't say "just wish and it comes true."

Instead, we'll show you how to use your brain's power in a real, practical way.

Summary

- This book is about truth, not hype.
- You'll learn both the science and the myths.
- By the end, you'll know exactly how manifestation works — and how to use it.

✦✦✦

PART 2

Basics of Affirmations

Chapter 6 – What Are Affirmations?

Affirmations are **short, powerful statements** that you repeat to yourself to influence your thoughts and beliefs.

For example:

- "I am confident."
- "I am improving every day."
- "I deserve success."

At first glance, affirmations may look silly or too simple. But they're actually a tool for **mental reprogramming.**

Why Words Matter

Your brain is like a sponge. Whatever you tell it repeatedly, it starts to believe.

Think about it:

- If someone keeps telling you, “You’re lazy, you’re useless,” after a while, you’ll start to feel it’s true.
- If someone keeps telling you, “You’re capable, you’re hardworking,” you’ll start to feel stronger and more confident.

The words you tell yourself daily matter more than the words others tell you.

The Inner Dialogue

We all have a voice in our head. Sometimes it encourages us, sometimes it criticizes us.

- “I can’t do this.”
- “I’ll never get better.”
- “I’m so stupid.”

This is called **negative self-talk.**

If repeated enough, it becomes your belief system.

Affirmations are simply a way to **flip that dialogue** into something empowering.

Example

- A job seeker keeps thinking: "I'll never get hired." → He shows up to interviews nervous, doubtful, and underconfident.
- Another job seeker thinks: "I have valuable skills, and I'll find the right job." → He shows up calm, speaks confidently, and gets hired.

The situation is the same, but the belief changed the outcome.

Practical Exercise

Take a sheet of paper.

1. Write down 5 negative thoughts you often have about yourself.
2. Flip them into positive affirmations.
   - "I am not confident" → "I am building confidence every day."

  - "I fail at everything" → "I learn and improve with every step."

Repeat these daily for 30 days and observe how your mood and actions shift.

Summary

- Affirmations = positive self-talk to reprogram the mind.
- Words influence beliefs → beliefs shape actions → actions shape results.
- Flipping negative thoughts into affirmations creates powerful change.

✦✦✦

Chapter 7 – How the Brain Processes Repeated Thoughts

Why do affirmations need repetition?

Because your brain learns through **repetition and patterns.**

The Science of Repetition

Your brain is made up of billions of neurons (nerve cells).

- Every thought you think creates a tiny electrical connection.
- When you repeat a thought, that connection gets stronger.
- Eventually, it becomes a **neural pathway.**

This is called **neuroplasticity** — the brain's ability to rewire itself.

So if you keep repeating:

- "I'm a failure" → that belief gets stronger.
- "I'm capable" → that belief also gets stronger.

👉 Whatever you repeat becomes your "mental truth."

Analogy: Walking a Path

Imagine a grassy field. If you walk across it once, nothing much changes. But if you walk the same path every day, eventually the grass flattens, and a clear trail forms.

That's how repeated thoughts work in the brain. The more you repeat them, the stronger the "mental trail."

Example: Language Learning

How do people learn a new language? By repeating words daily. At first it feels difficult, but over time, the brain wires itself to recognize and use those words naturally.

Affirmations work the same way. They "teach" your brain to think in a new language — the language of confidence, patience, and success.

Practical Exercise

Pick one affirmation that matters to you right now.
Example: *"I am consistent with my goals."*

Say it:

- Morning (right after waking up).
- Night (just before sleep).
- Whenever you catch yourself doubting.

Stick with one for at least 21–30 days. This is how the brain builds a new pathway.

Summary

- Brain learns through repetition (neuroplasticity).
- Thoughts create mental pathways, repeated ones become strong.

- Affirmations are like teaching your brain a new language.

✦✦✦

Chapter 8 – Positive Self-Talk vs Negative Self-Talk

Every day, you talk to yourself — in your head. This self-talk can be your greatest strength or your biggest weakness.

Negative Self-Talk

- "I can't do this."
- "I'm not good enough."
- "I always fail."

When you repeat such thoughts, your brain starts to believe them, and you act accordingly. This creates a **downward spiral.**

Positive Self-Talk

- "I'm learning step by step."
- "I deserve good things."
- "I can handle challenges."

Positive self-talk doesn't mean lying to yourself. It means focusing on possibilities instead of limits.

Example: Athlete in Training

- Athlete A: Keeps saying, "I'm too slow, I'll never win." He loses motivation and performs poorly.
- Athlete B: Says, "I'm improving daily." He trains harder, sees progress, and eventually wins.

The same training, but different inner voices = different outcomes.

Why It Matters Scientifically

Negative self-talk increases stress hormones like **cortisol.** Positive self-talk increases motivation chemicals like **dopamine and serotonin.**

So your body literally performs differently depending on your self-talk.

Practical Exercise

Step 1: Catch yourself. Write down 3 negative phrases you say often.
Step 2: Rewrite them into positive alternatives.
Step 3: Replace them instantly whenever they show up in your head.

Over time, your brain learns the new pattern.

Summary

- Negative self-talk creates failure loops.
- Positive self-talk builds resilience and motivation.
- Your brain and body react to the type of words you use.

✦✦✦

Chapter 9 – Why Simple Repetition Isn't Enough

Some people say affirmations don't work. Why? Because repetition alone is not enough.

The Missing Ingredients

1. **Emotion** – Saying "I am successful" without feeling it is like writing words on water. You need emotion to imprint it in your brain.
2. **Action** – Affirmations must lead to action. You can't say "I'm fit" while eating junk food all day.
3. **Believability** – If the statement feels fake, your brain rejects it. Example: Saying "I'm a millionaire" when you're broke creates inner resistance.

How to Fix It

- Use **realistic but powerful affirmations.**
  Example: Instead of "I am a millionaire," say "I am learning and building financial success."
- Add **emotion.** Visualize what it feels like when it's true.
- Take **small actions daily.** Affirmations set the mindset, actions create the result.

Example: Public Speaking Fear

- Wrong way: "I'm the best speaker in the world" → brain says "No you're not."
- Right way: "I'm improving as a speaker every time I practice." → brain accepts, confidence grows with action.

Practical Exercise

Pick one area you struggle with.
Write one realistic, believable affirmation about it.

Example: "I am learning to manage my time better." Now, pair it with one small daily action (using a planner, setting reminders, etc.).

Summary

- Repetition alone isn't enough.
- Affirmations must include **emotion + action + believability.**
- The right formula = believable words + daily practice.

✦✦✦

Chapter 10 – The Science of Belief Formation

Why do affirmations eventually work? Because they shape **beliefs.**

How Beliefs Are Formed

- You experience something.
- You think about it repeatedly.
- Your brain accepts it as "truth."
- You act according to it.

Beliefs are not always facts. They are simply **repeated thoughts + experiences.**

Example: Childhood Messages

- A child always told, “You’re smart” → grows up confident.
- A child always told, “You’re stupid” → grows up doubting themselves.

Neither is the full truth, but the belief becomes reality.

Affirmations as Belief Tools

By consciously repeating empowering statements, you create new beliefs. Over time, these override old negative ones.

- Old belief: “I always fail.”
- New belief: “I learn and improve every time.”

Once the new belief is installed, your actions align with it.

Practical Exercise

Ask yourself:

1. What belief is holding me back?
2. What belief do I want instead?

3. What affirmation will help me build it?

Then repeat it for 30–60 days with emotion and action.

Summary

- Beliefs are repeated thoughts, not always facts.
- Childhood experiences create powerful beliefs.
- Affirmations can build new, empowering beliefs.

✦✦✦

PART 3

Psychology of Belief

Chapter 11 – How Beliefs Shape Behavior

Every action you take in life starts with a belief — whether you realize it or not.

👉 If you believe something is possible, you act with confidence.

👉 If you believe something is impossible, you don't even try.

This is why two people in the same situation can behave so differently.

The Belief → Behavior → Result Loop

1. **Belief:** "I can improve my health."

2. **Behavior:** You exercise, eat better, and stay consistent.
3. **Result:** Health improves → belief gets stronger.

On the other side:

1. **Belief:** "Nothing will help me."
2. **Behavior:** You avoid exercise, eat poorly.
3. **Result:** Health worsens → negative belief gets stronger.

Your beliefs create your behaviors, and your behaviors reinforce your beliefs. This loop can either **lift you up** or **hold you down.**

Example: Business Owner

- Owner A believes "The market is full of opportunities." → He experiments, markets aggressively, and finds success.
- Owner B believes "The economy is dead." → He avoids risks, stops innovating, and struggles.

The market is the same, but belief shaped the behavior → which shaped the outcome.

Science Insight: Cognitive Bias

Psychologists call this **confirmation bias** — once you believe something, you unconsciously look for evidence to prove it true.

- Believe "people are kind"? You'll notice helpful strangers.
- Believe "people are cruel"? You'll notice rude strangers.

Your brain works like a lawyer, always trying to prove your belief right.

Practical Exercise

Write down one negative belief you have about yourself or your future.
Now, ask:

- What behaviors does this belief make me avoid?
- What would I do differently if I believed the opposite?

Then, take one small action as if the positive belief was already true.

Summary

- Beliefs drive behaviors, behaviors create results.
- Confirmation bias makes beliefs stronger.
- Changing behavior (even small steps) can slowly shift beliefs.

✦✦✦

Chapter 12 – The Role of the Subconscious Mind

Most of our beliefs are not stored in the "thinking" part of the brain but in the **subconscious mind.**

What is the Subconscious?

- The conscious mind = logical, decision-making (about 5–10% of your thoughts).
- The subconscious = habits, emotions, automatic programs (90–95% of your thoughts).

👉 Example: When you first learned to drive, you had to think about every move. Now, you drive almost automatically. That's your subconscious at work.

Why Affirmations Target the Subconscious

Affirmations are repeated to **install new programs** in the subconscious.

- At first, your conscious mind may resist: "This isn't true."
- But with repetition, the subconscious begins to accept it.

That's why affirmations need time. They're reprogramming old habits of thought.

Example: Fear of Public Speaking

- Conscious thought: "I want to speak confidently."
- Subconscious program: "Speaking is scary, I'll embarrass myself."

Unless you reprogram the subconscious, the fear dominates. Affirmations, combined with practice, slowly change the subconscious pattern.

Practical Exercise

Before sleep (when the conscious mind relaxes), repeat 3 affirmations you want your subconscious to absorb.
Example:

- “I speak with calm confidence.”
- “I handle challenges with clarity.”
- “I am improving every day.”

Do this nightly for 30 days and notice changes.

Summary

- Subconscious controls most behavior.
- Affirmations work by reprogramming the subconscious.
- Repetition at relaxed times (like before sleep) is most effective.

✦✦✦

Chapter 13 – Cognitive Dissonance: Why Our Mind Resists Change

When you first try affirmations, your mind often fights back. This is called **cognitive dissonance.**

What Is Cognitive Dissonance?

It's the discomfort you feel when your beliefs and your actions don't match.

- Example: You say "I'm confident," but you *feel* nervous. Your brain says, "This doesn't add up."

This discomfort is why many people quit affirmations early.

Why Resistance Happens

The brain likes familiarity, even if it's negative.

- If you've believed "I'm not good enough" for years, that belief feels safe and familiar.
- A new belief feels strange, so the brain rejects it at first.

How to Overcome It

1. Start with **believable affirmations.**
    - Instead of "I'm rich," say "I'm learning to manage money better."
2. Pair words with **action.**
    - When actions prove the affirmation true, the brain slowly accepts it.
3. Allow **time.**
    - Just like exercise, mental rewiring takes consistency.

Example: Fitness Journey

- Saying "I'm fit" while being unhealthy feels fake.

- Saying "I'm becoming fitter each week" feels believable.
- As you exercise, results show → the brain starts believing.

Practical Exercise

Pick one affirmation that currently feels "unbelievable." Rewrite it in a softer, believable way. Example:

- From "I'm successful" → "I'm building habits that lead to success."

Repeat daily and take small actions that prove it true.

Summary

- Cognitive dissonance = mental resistance to new beliefs.
- Start with believable affirmations.
- Pair with action to reduce resistance.

✦✦✦

Chapter 14 – How Beliefs Influence Confidence

Confidence is not just a personality trait. It is largely built on **beliefs.**

Belief → Confidence → Action

- If you believe you *can* do something, you feel confident, and you act boldly.
- If you believe you *cannot*, you hesitate, and your actions are weak.

Example: Job Interview

- Candidate A believes "I'm not good enough." → Nervous, poor body language, weak answers.

- Candidate B believes “I have valuable skills.” → Calm, clear answers, confident posture.

Both may have the same qualifications, but belief shaped confidence, and confidence shaped performance.

Science Insight: Self-Efficacy

Psychologist Albert Bandura introduced **self-efficacy** — the belief in your own ability to succeed.
High self-efficacy → more resilience, better performance.
Low self-efficacy → avoidance, quick failure.

Practical Exercise

Think of one area where you lack confidence.
Write down 3 skills or actions you *already* do well in that area.
Turn them into affirmations:

- “I prepare well for presentations.”
- “I answer questions clearly.”
- “I improve with every practice.”

This builds belief → which builds confidence.

Summary

- Confidence is belief in your own ability.
- Beliefs strongly influence confidence levels.
- Affirmations can boost self-efficacy by focusing on strengths.

✦✦✦

Chapter 15 – Self-Image and Identity Formation

Your beliefs don’t just shape actions — they shape your entire **identity.**

What is Self-Image?

Self-image = how you see yourself.

- “I’m smart.”
- “I’m lazy.”
- “I’m unlucky.”

Whatever identity you repeat becomes your truth.

Why Identity Matters More than Goals

If you set a goal but your self-image doesn't match, you'll sabotage yourself.

- Goal: "I want to exercise daily."
- Self-image: "I'm lazy." → You skip workouts.

But if you shift identity:

- New self-image: "I'm a healthy person." → You act like one naturally.

Example: Smoker Trying to Quit

- Person A: Says, "I'm trying to quit smoking." → Identity = still a smoker.
- Person B: Says, "I don't smoke anymore." → Identity = non-smoker.

Same goal, but identity shift makes a huge difference.

How Affirmations Shape Identity

Affirmations repeated daily create a new self-image. Over time, this identity becomes automatic.

- Old identity: "I'm always broke."

- New identity: “I’m learning to manage money wisely.”
- Actions follow identity → better results.

Practical Exercise

Write down 3 negative self-identities you currently hold.
Example: “I’m lazy,” “I’m shy,” “I’m unlucky.”
Rewrite them into positive identity affirmations:

- “I’m disciplined and improving daily.”
- “I’m confident in social situations.”
- “I attract opportunities.”

Repeat until the new self-image feels natural.

Summary

- Self-image is your identity shaped by beliefs.
- Goals fail without identity alignment.
- Affirmations are powerful tools for identity change.

✦✦✦

PART 4

Neuroscience of Affirmations & Manifestation

Chapter 16 – Neuroplasticity: The Brain's Ability to Change

For a long time, scientists believed the brain was "fixed" after childhood. But now we know something amazing: the brain can change at any age. This ability is called **neuroplasticity.**

What is Neuroplasticity?

- "Neuro" = brain cells (neurons).
- "Plasticity" = flexibility or ability to reshape.

Neuroplasticity means your brain can rewire itself by forming new connections between neurons.

👉 *Every time you learn a new skill, change a habit, or think differently, you are literally reshaping your brain.*

How Affirmations Use Neuroplasticity

- When you repeat an affirmation, it fires a set of neurons.
- With repetition, those neurons form stronger connections.
- The brain begins to accept this as a "new truth."

This is why affirmations don't work instantly. You're not just saying words — you're **rewiring your brain.**

Analogy: Dirt Road to Highway

Imagine a forest.

- A rarely walked path is narrow and overgrown.
- If people walk there daily, it becomes a clear trail.
- If cars start driving there daily, it becomes a wide road.

That's what affirmations do to your brain — they turn weak thought paths into strong highways.

Practical Exercise

Pick one affirmation. Repeat it **daily for at least 30 days.** Notice:

- In the first week, it feels strange.
- By the third week, it feels normal.
- By the sixth week, it starts influencing your actions.

That's neuroplasticity in action.

Summary

- Brain is not fixed; it can rewire itself (neuroplasticity).
- Affirmations build new neural pathways.
- Repetition and time are key for rewiring.

✦✦✦

Chapter 17 – The Reticular Activating System (RAS): Your Brain's Filter

Your brain is bombarded with millions of bits of information every second. But you only notice a tiny part of it.

The **Reticular Activating System (RAS)** is the brain's filter. It decides what you pay attention to.

Everyday Example

- You buy a red car → suddenly you see red cars everywhere.
- A pregnant woman → suddenly notices baby products and other pregnant women everywhere.

Those things were always there, but your RAS started noticing them because they became important to you.

How Affirmations Use the RAS

When you repeat an affirmation, you train your RAS to look for opportunities that match it.

- Affirmation: "I attract opportunities to grow in my career."
- RAS effect: You notice job openings, mentors, learning chances that you previously ignored.

It doesn't "magically" bring opportunities. It simply helps your brain **spot them faster**.

Analogy: Searchlight

Your RAS is like a flashlight in the dark. Whatever you focus on gets lit up. Affirmations direct the flashlight toward positive possibilities instead of negative fears.

Practical Exercise

For 7 days, repeat an affirmation like: *"I notice opportunities that help me grow."*
Then write down daily any opportunity you spotted — big or small. You'll be surprised how many were already around you.

Summary

- RAS = brain's filter for attention.
- Affirmations tune your RAS to notice matching opportunities.
- What you focus on, you see more of.

✦✦✦

Chapter 18 – The Role of Emotions in Brain Wiring

Affirmations are not just about words. **Emotion is the fuel** that makes them stick.

Why Emotion Matters

The brain pays special attention to emotional experiences.

- That's why you remember your happiest or saddest days more than random ones.
- Emotion makes the brain release chemicals (like dopamine) that strengthen memory and learning.

So, saying "I am confident" without emotion is weak. Saying it while **feeling** confidence makes the brain treat it as real.

Example: Sports Visualization

Athletes don't just say, "I'll win." They **visualize** the win, feel the excitement, hear the crowd, sense the victory. The brain processes this almost like a real experience, making performance better in reality.

How to Add Emotion to Affirmations

1. **Visualize** the outcome — see it in your mind like a movie.
2. **Feel it** — imagine the excitement, pride, or peace you'd feel.
3. **Use your body** — say it with energy, stand tall, breathe deeply.

Practical Exercise

Take one affirmation. Instead of saying it flatly, close your eyes and imagine it fully. Example:

- Affirmation: "I am calm and confident on stage."
- Visualization: Imagine yourself on stage, smiling, speaking smoothly, hearing applause.

- Emotion: Feel the confidence spreading through your body.

Summary

- Emotion makes affirmations powerful.
- Brain remembers emotional experiences strongly.
- Visualizing + feeling = faster brain rewiring.

✦✦✦

Chapter 19 – Why Habits Strengthen Affirmations

Affirmations prepare the mind, but **habits lock them in place.**

Affirmations Without Habits = Weak

- Saying "I'm healthy" while eating junk food confuses the brain.
- Saying "I'm confident" without practicing confidence feels fake.

Habits give affirmations proof. Proof convinces the brain.

Example: Learning Guitar

- Affirmation: “I’m a skilled guitarist.”
- Habit: Practicing 30 minutes daily.
- Result: Progress proves the affirmation true → belief grows stronger.

Science Insight: Habit Loops

Habits form through a loop:

1. **Cue** (trigger) → 2. **Routine** (action) → 3. **Reward** (feeling).

Affirmations can become part of the cue. Example:

- Cue: Morning alarm.
- Routine: Repeat affirmations.
- Reward: Feeling focused and motivated.

Over time, this becomes automatic.

Practical Exercise

Pick one affirmation and link it to a daily habit. Example:

- While brushing teeth: “I’m grateful for my health.”

- Before starting work: “I focus with clarity.”

This consistency locks affirmations into your subconscious.

Summary

- Habits + affirmations = strong belief.
- Habits act as proof that affirmations are true.
- Linking affirmations to daily routines makes them automatic.

✦✦✦

Chapter 20 – Brain Chemistry: Dopamine, Serotonin & Motivation

Your brain doesn't just run on thoughts — it runs on **chemicals**. These chemicals affect mood, motivation, and belief.

Key Brain Chemicals in Affirmations

1. **Dopamine** – the "reward chemical." Boosts motivation and goal pursuit.
   - Saying affirmations with action gives dopamine spikes.

2. **Serotonin** – the "happiness chemical." Increases self-esteem and stability.
    - Affirmations about gratitude or self-worth increase serotonin.
3. **Cortisol** – the "stress chemical." Too much reduces confidence.
    - Negative self-talk increases cortisol.
    - Positive affirmations reduce it, keeping you calmer.

Why This Matters

Your words literally change your brain chemistry. That's why affirmations can lift mood, reduce stress, and improve focus when practiced consistently.

Example: Morning Routine

- Person A wakes up and says: "Ugh, another terrible day." → Cortisol rises, mood drops.

- Person B wakes up and says: "I'm grateful for today's opportunities." → Dopamine and serotonin rise, energy increases.

Same morning, but brain chemistry creates different outcomes.

Practical Exercise

Start your day with 3 affirmations that target brain chemistry:

1. Gratitude (boosts serotonin): "I'm thankful for my health."
2. Confidence (boosts dopamine): "I'm capable of handling today's tasks."
3. Calmness (lowers cortisol): "I face challenges with peace and clarity."

Summary

- Brain chemicals influence mood and motivation.
- Affirmations affect dopamine, serotonin, and cortisol.

- Daily affirmations can re-balance brain chemistry for success.

✦✦✦

PART 5

Law of Attraction: Science vs Myth

Chapter 21 – Origins of the Law of Attraction

The **Law of Attraction (LoA)** is one of the most popular ideas in self-help. But where did it come from?

Historical Roots

- **Ancient Philosophy:** Hinduism and Buddhism spoke of karma and the power of thought thousands of years ago.
- **19th Century:** New Thought Movement (USA) spread ideas like "thoughts create reality."
- **2006:** The book and film *The Secret* made LoA famous worldwide, promising that you can "attract" anything with your thoughts.

The Core Idea

LoA claims:

- Thoughts are like magnets.
- Whatever you focus on (positive or negative) gets "attracted" into your life.

Why People Loved It

- It gave hope — "I can change my future with my thoughts."
- It was simple — no hard science or effort explained.
- It promised quick success — health, wealth, love.

But is it *true science* or just *motivational sugar*?

Practical Reflection

Think: Have you ever strongly wished for something and eventually got it?

- Was it magic?

- Or did your focus + action slowly align to make it happen?

We'll explore this in the next chapters.

Summary

- LoA has ancient roots but became mainstream with *The Secret*.
- Claims thoughts are magnetic.
- Popular because it's simple and hopeful.
- But we must test if it's real science.

✦✦✦

Chapter 22 – The Popular Claims of LoA

LoA teachers often make three main promises. Let's examine them.

Claim 1: "Thoughts are Vibrations"

They say thoughts send vibrations to the universe, which responds by sending matching experiences.

Problem: Science has no proof that thoughts "vibrate" into the cosmos.

- Yes, brain waves exist, but they don't leave your skull to rearrange the universe.
- Thoughts influence *you*, not the external cosmos directly.

Claim 2: "Ask, Believe, Receive"

Process taught in LoA:

1. Ask (decide what you want).
2. Believe (act as if you already have it).
3. Receive (it will show up).

Problem: Missing step = *Action*. Without action, nothing changes.

Claim 3: "You Attract What You Fear"

They say if you fear something, you invite it into your life.

Partial Truth:

- Fear keeps your brain focused on danger.
- That focus can influence decisions → leading to bad outcomes.
- But it's not mystical "attraction," it's psychology.

Practical Exercise

Write down one "LoA claim" you believed in. Ask yourself:

- Is there scientific evidence?
- Or is it psychology + action that explains it better?

Summary

- LoA promises: thoughts vibrate, ask-believe-receive, attract fear.
- Science shows no vibrations leave the brain.
- Psychology explains results better than "universe attraction."

✦✦✦

Chapter 23 – The Science Behind Attraction (What's Actually True)

Now let's separate fact from myth.

What's True in LoA

1. **Focus shapes perception (RAS):**
   - If you focus on opportunities, you notice them.
   - That feels like "attraction," but it's brain filtering.
2. **Belief shapes behavior:**

    - If you believe you'll succeed, you act confidently.
    - Confidence increases chances of success.

3. **Visualization trains the brain:**
    - Athletes practice mentally → their brain reacts as if they're doing it physically.

What's False in LoA

- Thoughts don't physically change external reality.
- The "universe" isn't arranging events just for you.
- You can't just sit and "receive" without action.

Analogy: GPS Navigation

- LoA says: Just imagine the destination, and the car drives itself.
- Reality: You must drive. The GPS (your focus) shows the path, but *you move the car.*

Practical Exercise

Pick a goal.

- Write an affirmation about it.
- Spend 2 minutes visualizing success.
- Then write **3 small actions** you can take today.

This combines the *real science* with practical steps.

Summary

- LoA works partly because of brain science: RAS, confidence, visualization.
- It fails when seen as magic.
- Real success = mental focus + consistent action.

✦✦✦

Chapter 24 – Why the "Magical" LoA Doesn't Work

Many people say: "I tried LoA, but nothing happened." Why?

Reason 1: Passive Waiting

They "asked" the universe but didn't act. Without behavior change, no results.

Reason 2: Unrealistic Expectations

LoA promotes: "Think it, and it appears fast." Reality takes time, discipline, and setbacks.

Reason 3: Confirmation Bias Only

Sometimes small coincidences happen, and people say "LoA worked."
But they ignore the times it didn't work. This is selective thinking.

Reason 4: Emotional Damage

When it fails, people blame themselves: "Maybe I didn't believe enough."
This creates guilt and low self-worth.

Example: Lottery Mindset

- LoA follower: "I'll attract lottery money."
- Reality: Odds are millions-to-one. Belief doesn't change math.
- When they lose, they feel like failures.

Practical Exercise

Instead of asking, "Why didn't the universe give me this?"
Ask, "What action did I skip?"

Summary

- Magical LoA fails due to passivity, unrealistic hopes, and bias.
- It can harm self-esteem.
- Real progress needs active effort.

✦✦✦

Chapter 25 – What Actually Works Instead of LoA

Now, let's present the **science-backed alternative.**

The Real Formula: Thought → Emotion → Action → Result

1. **Thought:** Affirmation sets focus.
2. **Emotion:** Visualization adds feeling.
3. **Action:** Small daily habits build momentum.
4. **Result:** Consistent outcomes appear.

This is not magic. It's psychology + neuroscience + discipline.

The Role of "Attraction" in Real Life

- When you think positively → You feel motivated.
- When motivated → You take more chances.
- When you take more chances → Success feels like "attraction."

So, the "universe" didn't give it — **you created it** by aligning thoughts, emotions, and actions.

Practical 3-Step Method

1. **Daily Affirmation:** "I focus on growth opportunities."
2. **Visualization:** Imagine yourself succeeding in one area.
3. **Action Step:** Take at least one small action daily (apply, call, practice, learn).

Case Study: Career Growth

- LoA believer: Says, "I'll attract promotion." Waits passively.

- Science-based person: Says, "I'm building skills for promotion." Learns, networks, takes initiatives.
- Result: The second person actually gets promoted.

Summary

- Instead of LoA magic, focus on the Thought → Emotion → Action → Result cycle.
- Positive mindset helps, but action is the engine.
- Success is created, not attracted.

✦✦✦

PART 6

Placebo Effect & Self-Healing

Chapter 26 – What is the Placebo Effect?

The **placebo effect** is one of the most fascinating discoveries in medicine.

Imagine this:

- A doctor gives two patients sugar pills (with no real medicine).
- Patient A is told, “This will reduce your pain.”
- Patient B is told nothing special.

Strangely, Patient A often reports **less pain** even though the pill had no active drug. Why?

👉 That’s the placebo effect: **when belief in a treatment creates real physical improvement.**

How It Works

1. **Expectation:** Patient expects relief.
2. **Brain Response:** Brain releases endorphins (natural painkillers).
3. **Body Response:** Pain signals reduce → patient feels better.

Real-Life Examples

- In clinical trials, patients on placebo sometimes improve almost as much as those on actual medicine.
- Placebos work best for **pain, stress, depression, and anxiety** — conditions where the brain strongly influences the body.

Why This Matters for Manifestation

The placebo effect shows that:

- Belief changes biology.

- The mind is powerful enough to trigger healing responses.

But — it has limits. Placebo can reduce pain, but it can't cure cancer or fix a broken bone.

Summary

- Placebo = fake treatment causing real improvement.
- Works through expectation + brain chemistry.
- Proof that belief affects the body, but with limits.

✦✦✦

Chapter 27 – The Science of Belief in Healing

Your body and brain are deeply connected.

Psychoneuroimmunology

This field studies how **thoughts and emotions influence the immune system.**

- Stress weakens immunity.
- Optimism and calmness strengthen immunity.

So belief isn't just "in the head." It literally affects your body's defense system.

Case Study: Recovery After Surgery

- Patients with positive beliefs ("I'll recover fast") heal quicker than those with fear and doubt.
- Why? Lower stress hormones → faster cell repair.

Example: Meditation & Healing

Studies show regular meditation:

- Lowers blood pressure.
- Reduces inflammation.
- Boosts immunity.

This isn't magic — it's biology responding to a calmer, more positive state.

Practical Exercise

Each night, before sleep, repeat:

- "My body knows how to heal."
- "Every cell is working for my recovery."

Combine this with deep breathing. You'll feel calmer, sleep better, and indirectly support healing.

Summary

- Belief affects health via stress and immune system.
- Positive mindset speeds recovery.
  - Calmness + faith = better healing environment.

✦✦✦

Chapter 28 – The Limits of Self-Healing

While belief is powerful, it's **not a replacement for medicine.**

What Self-Healing Can Do

- Reduce stress and pain.
- Boost immunity.
- Speed up recovery after illness.
- Improve mental health.

What It Cannot Do

- Cure serious diseases like cancer, diabetes, or infections.
- Replace surgery or antibiotics.
- “Manifest away” genetic disorders.

👉 Belief is a **supporting tool, not a miracle cure.**

Danger of Over-Belief

Some gurus say: “You don’t need doctors, just believe.” This is dangerous because patients may avoid real treatment, making illness worse.

Balanced Approach

- Use belief + affirmations to stay positive.
- But always combine with medical treatment.

Analogy: Car Repair

- Belief = keeping the car clean, fueled, and well-maintained.

- Medicine = fixing broken parts with tools.

  Both are needed for smooth driving.

Summary

- Self-healing works for stress, immunity, recovery.
- Doesn't replace real medicine.
- Use belief as support, not as the only solution.

✦✦✦

Chapter 29 – Mind-Body Practices That Boost Healing

Some practices naturally combine belief, calmness, and body health.

---

1. Meditation

- Calms the mind → lowers cortisol.
- Increases brain's healing capacity.

2. Yoga & Breathwork

- Reduces stress.
- Improves circulation.
- Enhances mind-body awareness.

3. Visualization

- Patients imagining immune cells fighting disease showed stronger recovery in studies.

4. Gratitude Journaling

- Improves mood.
- Reduces stress.
- Strengthens optimism, which boosts health.

Example: Cancer Patients Using Visualization

Some patients imagine white blood cells "attacking" cancer cells. While it doesn't cure cancer alone, it helps patients stay calmer and improves treatment response.

Practical Exercise

Try this 5-minute healing visualization:

1. Close your eyes.
2. Breathe deeply.
3. Imagine a warm golden light spreading in your body, repairing every cell.
4. Say: *"My body is healing with every breath."*

Summary

- Meditation, yoga, visualization, gratitude all support healing.
- They reduce stress and strengthen immune system.
- Great as complementary practices.

✦✦✦

Chapter 30 – The Placebo Effect and Manifestation: The Connection

Now let's connect everything.

How Placebo & Manifestation Are Similar

1. Both rely on **belief.**
2. Both trigger **brain chemistry changes.**
3. Both influence **how the body and mind act.**

The Key Difference

- Placebo = external trigger (a pill, treatment, ritual).

- Manifestation = internal trigger (affirmation, visualization).

Both change your mindset → mindset changes biology → biology changes results.

Why This Is Proof Manifestation Works (Partially)

- If belief can reduce pain (placebo), belief can also increase confidence (manifestation).
- But just like placebo has limits, manifestation has limits too.

Practical Integration

Next time you set a manifestation goal:

- Treat affirmations like a "placebo pill."
- Fully believe in them.
- Combine with real action.

The belief will strengthen your brain's response, just like in placebo healing.

Summary

- Placebo and manifestation both rely on belief.
- They prove the mind can influence body and life.
- But both have limits — belief works best with action.

✦✦✦

PART 7

Psychology of Positive Thinking

Chapter 31 – What is Positive Thinking Really?

When people hear "positive thinking," many imagine fake smiles, ignoring problems, or blindly repeating happy phrases. That's **not** what real positive thinking means.

👉 Real positive thinking = **choosing a mindset of possibility and growth, even in difficulties.**

Breaking the Misconception

- **Fake version:** "Everything is perfect, I have no problems." (denial)
- **Real version:** "Yes, challenges exist, but I'll focus on solutions instead of only problems." (empowerment)

Psychology Definition

In psychology, positive thinking is linked to:

- **Optimism** (expecting good outcomes).
- **Resilience** (bouncing back after setbacks).
- **Hope** (believing effort can improve future).

Example: Two Job Seekers

- **Negative thinker:** "No company will hire me." → applies half-heartedly → gives up after rejection.
- **Positive thinker:** "I'll keep learning and trying." → applies confidently → improves skills → eventually hired.

Same environment, different mindset, different results.

Practical Reflection

Think about a time you faced failure. Did your mindset pull you down, or push you forward? That's the power of positive thinking.

Summary

- Positive thinking isn't denial; it's solution-focused.
- It includes optimism, resilience, and hope.
- Mindset changes how you act, and how results turn out.

✦✦✦

Chapter 32 – The Science of Optimism

Scientists have studied optimism for decades. Results are clear: optimistic people generally live healthier, happier, and more successful lives.

Physical Health Benefits

- Optimists recover faster after surgery.
- They have lower risk of heart disease.
- They even live longer on average.

👉 Why? Optimism reduces stress, and stress hormones are damaging long-term.

Mental Health Benefits

- Optimists experience less depression.
- They cope with setbacks better.
- They see failures as temporary, not permanent.

Study Example

A study tracked students for 25 years. Those with higher optimism in college had:

- Better health.
- More stable careers.
- More satisfaction in relationships.

The "Explanatory Style"

Optimists explain events differently than pessimists:

- Optimist: "This is temporary, and I can improve it."
- Pessimist: "This is permanent, and I'm helpless."

That single difference changes everything.

Practical Exercise

Next time something bad happens, write down:

1. Is this permanent or temporary?
2. Is it fully my fault, or are there outside factors?
3. What small step can I take?

This rewires your brain toward optimism.

Summary

- Optimism is proven to improve health, success, and happiness.
- Optimists explain failures as temporary and controllable.
- You can train optimism with practice.

✦✦✦

Chapter 33 – Positive Thinking vs Toxic Positivity

Not all positivity is good. Sometimes it becomes **toxic positivity.**

What is Toxic Positivity?

It's when people force positivity and deny real struggles. Examples:

- Saying "Just be happy" to someone with depression.
- Pretending everything is fine while suffering inside.

Why It's Harmful

- Suppresses real emotions.

- Makes people feel guilty for being sad.
- Prevents real problem-solving.

Healthy Positivity vs Toxic Positivity

- **Healthy:** "I'm struggling, but I'll find ways to handle it."
- **Toxic:** "I'm not allowed to feel sad or angry."

Example: Breakup

- Toxic: "I must smile and act like I'm over it instantly."
- Healthy: "It hurts, but I'll heal and grow stronger from this."

Practical Tip

Allow yourself to feel emotions first. Then, once you process them, shift to solution-focused thinking.

Summary

- Positive thinking is good, but forced positivity is toxic.
- Acknowledge emotions, don't suppress them.
    - Balance: feel → accept → focus on growth.

✦✦✦

Chapter 34 – How Positive Thinking Shapes Behavior

Your mindset doesn't just affect how you *feel*. It changes how you *act*.

The Cycle of Thought → Behavior → Result

1. **Thought:** "I can learn this skill."
2. **Behavior:** You practice daily.
3. **Result:** Skill improves.

Now reverse it:

1. **Thought:** "I'm not smart enough."
2. **Behavior:** You avoid practice.
3. **Result:** You fail → belief becomes stronger.

This is called a **self-fulfilling prophecy.**

Example: Public Speaking

- Negative thinker: "I'll embarrass myself." → avoids practice → stumbles on stage.
- Positive thinker: "I can improve." → practices → performs better.

Same starting point, different outcomes due to mindset.

Scientific Study

Students who believed intelligence can grow (growth mindset) studied harder and achieved higher grades than those who believed intelligence is fixed.

Practical Exercise

Write down one negative belief you hold (e.g., "I'm bad at money"). Replace it with:

- "I can improve my money skills step by step."
  Now, list one action to take this week.

Summary

- Positive thinking shapes behavior → behavior shapes results.
- Negative beliefs create self-fulfilling failure.
- Reframe belief → change actions → change life.

✦✦✦

Chapter 35 – Practical Exercises for Real Positivity

Now let's learn how to **practice positive thinking daily.**

---

1. Gratitude Journaling

Every night, write 3 things you're grateful for.

- Shifts focus from lack → abundance.
- Proven to improve happiness and reduce stress.

---

2. Reframing Practice

When a negative event happens, ask:

- "What can I learn from this?"
- "How can I grow stronger?"

---

3. Affirmations with Action

Say: "I am becoming more confident."
Then take one small action that builds confidence (e.g., speaking up once in a meeting).

---

4. Visualization Routine

Spend 2 minutes imagining yourself succeeding at one goal.
This trains your brain to believe it's possible.

---

5. Surround Yourself with Positivity

- People, books, media all influence mindset.
- Choose uplifting input instead of constant negativity.

Daily 5-Minute Routine

1. 1 minute gratitude.
2. 1 minute affirmation.

3. 1 minute visualization.

4. 1 minute breathing.

5. 1 minute action planning.

Summary

- Positivity is a practice, not luck.
- Gratitude, reframing, affirmations, visualization, and good environment all help.
- Small daily routines make positivity natural over time.

✦✦✦

PART 8

Affirmations & Brain Rewiring

Chapter 36 – What Are Affirmations?

At their simplest, **affirmations are positive statements you repeat to yourself to influence your mindset and behavior.**

Examples:

- "I am becoming more confident."
- "I deserve success and happiness."
- "I can handle challenges calmly."

Why Do People Use Them?

Affirmations are like mental reminders that:

- Direct your focus.

- Strengthen positive beliefs.
- Break negative self-talk cycles.

The Psychology of Self-Talk

We all have an inner voice. Sometimes it supports us: *"You can do this."* Other times it criticizes: *"You'll fail again."*

👉 Affirmations are a tool to **train that inner voice** toward encouragement instead of sabotage.

Example: Athlete Training

- Negative self-talk: "I'm not good enough to win." → low confidence → poor performance.
- Positive affirmation: "I've trained hard, I'm strong and ready." → boosted confidence → better performance.

Practical Tip

Start with simple daily affirmations like:

- "I am learning and growing each day."

- "I am stronger than my doubts."

Say them in the mirror every morning.

Summary

- Affirmations are positive self-talk tools.
- They replace negative inner dialogue with empowering thoughts.
- Used by athletes, students, professionals to build confidence.

✦✦✦

Chapter 37 – How Affirmations Rewire the Brain

Affirmations work because of **neuroplasticity** — the brain's ability to change its structure and connections based on repeated thoughts and experiences.

Neuroplasticity Explained Simply

- Imagine your brain like a forest.
- Each thought is like walking down a path.
- The more often you walk a path, the clearer and stronger it becomes.
- Affirmations are like **choosing to walk a positive path every day.**

Over time, the brain builds stronger "positive" pathways and weakens negative ones.

Scientific Backing

- Studies show affirmations activate the **reward centers of the brain** (ventromedial prefrontal cortex).
- They increase resilience during stress.
- MRI scans prove repeated affirmations create measurable changes in brain activity.

Example: Student Confidence

- Student with negative self-talk: "I always fail math."
- Student practicing affirmation: "I am learning math step by step, and I improve daily."

After weeks of repetition, the second student's brain starts associating math with growth instead of failure → leading to better effort and results.

Practical Exercise

Choose one negative belief you want to change.

- Negative: “I’m bad at public speaking.”
- Positive affirmation: “I am becoming a clear and confident speaker.”
  Repeat daily for 30 days. Notice how your comfort level grows.

Summary

- Affirmations use neuroplasticity to rewire brain pathways.
- Repetition strengthens positive thought circuits.
- Science confirms affirmations activate reward and resilience systems.

✦✦✦

Chapter 38 – Designing Effective Affirmations

Not all affirmations work. Many fail because they're unrealistic or vague.

Rules for Strong Affirmations

1. **Present Tense:** Say "I am" or "I'm becoming," not "I will."
    - ❌ "I will be confident someday."
    - ✅ "I am becoming confident now."
2. **Positive Language:** Avoid negatives.
    - ❌ "I'm not afraid."
    - ✅ "I am calm and strong."

3. **Believable Steps:** Make them realistic.
    - ❌ "I'm a millionaire overnight."
    - ✅ "I am improving my money skills every day."
4. **Emotional Connection:** Words should feel inspiring, not robotic.

Examples of Weak vs Strong Affirmations

- Weak: "I am rich." (feels fake if you're broke)
- Strong: "I am learning to manage money wisely."
- Weak: "I am perfect."
- Strong: "I am enough as I am, and I'm improving daily."

Practical Formula

"I am + (positive trait/action) + (in progress)."
Example: *"I am becoming more focused and productive each day."*

Summary

- Effective affirmations must be present, positive, believable, and emotional.
- Unrealistic affirmations backfire.
- Use a simple formula to design practical ones.

✦✦✦

Chapter 39 – Daily Practices for Brain Rewiring

Affirmations work best when practiced regularly and combined with actions.

Morning Mirror Routine

- Look into your eyes in the mirror.
- Say your top 3 affirmations out loud.
- Example: "I am capable, I am confident, I am focused."

Journaling Method

Write affirmations daily in a notebook.
Repetition through writing strengthens memory and belief.

Visualization Combo

Combine affirmations with mental pictures.

- Say: "I am confident."
- Visualize yourself speaking clearly on stage.

This double impact strengthens brain pathways faster.

Habit Stacking

Attach affirmations to daily habits.

- While brushing teeth → say affirmations.
- Before sleep → repeat them mentally.

Consistency is Key

Repeating affirmations once won't change anything. But doing them daily for weeks creates new neural patterns.

Summary

- Practice affirmations daily (mirror, journaling, visualization).
- Combine with habits for consistency.
- Regular repetition = brain rewiring.

Chapter 40 – Affirmations + Action = Real Change

Affirmations alone won't magically change your life. They're powerful, but only when combined with real effort.

The Danger of "Empty Affirmations"

Saying: "I am wealthy" → but never learning money skills = nothing changes.
Saying: "I am healthy" → but eating junk daily = no improvement.

👉 Affirmations without action = daydreaming.

The Power Combo

- Affirmation builds belief.

- Belief motivates action.
- Action creates results.

Example: Fitness Goal

- Affirmation: "I am becoming stronger and healthier."
- Action: Exercise + good food.
- Result: Fitness improves.

The affirmation fuels motivation, but action delivers the outcome.

Practical Formula for Any Goal

1. **Affirmation:** Positive belief statement.
2. **Micro-Action:** Small daily step.
3. **Review:** Notice progress weekly.

Case Study: Learning a New Skill

- Affirmation: "I am becoming skilled in programming."
- Daily Action: Practice coding for 30 minutes.
- After 6 months → real skill built.

Summary

- Affirmations must pair with action.
- Belief motivates, but action transforms.
- Use affirmations as fuel for consistent effort.

✦✦✦

PART 9

Law of Attraction: Science vs Myth

Chapter 41 – The Origins of the Law of Attraction

The **Law of Attraction (LOA)** is often marketed as:
"Think about what you want, and the universe will deliver it."

But where did this idea come from?

Historical Roots

- **Ancient philosophies:** Hinduism, Buddhism, and Stoicism all spoke about the power of thought and intention.
- **New Thought movement (1800s):** Western spiritual writers began claiming thoughts have magnetic power.

- **The Secret (2006):** A bestselling book/movie that popularized LOA worldwide with stories like "just visualize checks in the mail, and they'll arrive."

The Problem

People took it too literally. They believed:

- Think rich → money magically comes.
- Think healthy → disease disappears.

This gave LOA a reputation of being "pseudo-science."

Why People Believe It

1. **Confirmation bias:** When something good happens after thinking positively, people credit LOA.
2. **Placebo effect:** Belief alone can trigger real changes in the body.
3. **Hope marketing:** LOA promises quick results, which people naturally want.

Summary

- LOA started from old philosophies, spread through modern self-help.
- Popularized by *The Secret* in 2006.

Belief grew because of psychology effects, not magic.

✦✦✦

Chapter 42 – The Myth of "Ask, Believe, Receive"

The core LOA formula is: **Ask → Believe → Receive.**

Why It Sounds Attractive

- Easy. No effort needed.
- Gives hope to people feeling powerless.
- Feels like control over the universe.

The Myth

Unfortunately, science doesn't support the idea that simply "asking the universe" makes things appear.

- No evidence thoughts emit "magnetic waves" that attract physical objects.
- Sitting on the couch visualizing money won't make it fall from the sky.

The Reality

What actually works is:

- **Ask = Set a clear goal.**
- **Believe = Build confidence in yourself.**
- **Receive = Take action + notice opportunities.**

Example: Career Goal

- Myth version: Visualize promotion → universe delivers.
- Real version: Visualize → feel motivated → take more initiative → boss notices → promotion comes.

Summary

- "Ask, Believe, Receive" is misleading if taken literally.
- Visualization works, but only when followed by action.
- LOA is useful as a motivational tool, not a magic wand.

✦✦✦

Chapter 43 – The Science Behind Attraction

So, if not magic, why do people still see results from LOA? Because parts of it **are rooted in psychology and neuroscience.**

Key Scientific Concepts

1. **RAS (Reticular Activating System):**
    - Brain filter that notices what you focus on.
    - If you focus on wealth, you'll spot financial opportunities you ignored before.
2. **Neuroplasticity:**

    - Repeating affirmations and visualizations rewires brain circuits.
    - This changes confidence and behavior.

3. **Behavioral Activation:**
    - Positive thinking motivates people to take action, even small ones, that accumulate over time.

Study Example

- People who visualized studying well before exams → studied longer and scored higher.
- Not because of "attraction," but because visualization boosted motivation and effort.

Real-World Analogy

It's like wearing colored glasses:

- Negative glasses = you only see problems.
- Positive glasses = you notice chances to grow.

Summary

- LOA works through psychology, not magic.
- RAS, neuroplasticity, and motivation explain the "attraction effect."
- Science supports focus → awareness → action → results.

✦✦✦

Chapter 44 – Why the Law of Attraction Fails for Many

Not everyone succeeds with LOA. Why?

Reason 1 – Passive Wishing

People sit and wait, instead of acting.

- Example: Visualizing a business but never starting it.

Reason 2 – Unrealistic Expectations

LOA gurus say "anything is possible instantly," but reality requires time and effort.

- Example: Expecting a million-dollar cheque overnight.

Reason 3 – Ignoring Negative Emotions

Toxic positivity makes people suppress fear, anger, or sadness. This blocks growth.

Reason 4 – Lack of Clarity

Vague goals = vague results.

- Saying "I want success" is too general.
- Saying "I want to build a digital marketing career" gives direction.

Case Study: Two Entrepreneurs

- A believes LOA will bring customers magically → no marketing → business fails.
- B uses LOA as motivation + builds strategy → notices opportunities → business grows.

Summary

- LOA fails if used passively, unrealistically, or vaguely.
- It only works when paired with clear goals, effort, and emotional honesty.

✦✦✦

Chapter 45 – A Balanced View: What Actually Works

Now that myths are busted, what's the truth?

What LOA Really Means

- It's not "Universe is Amazon."
- It's your **brain and behavior aligning with focus.**

Formula for Real Attraction

1. **Clarity:** Define specific goals.
2. **Visualization:** Imagine success to boost confidence.
3. **Affirmation:** Replace doubt with belief.

4. **Action:** Take consistent steps.
5. **Openness:** Notice and grab opportunities.

Example: Fitness Transformation

- Old belief: "I can't lose weight." → gives up.
- New LOA approach:
    - Goal: Lose 10 kg in 6 months.
    - Visualization: Picture healthier self.
    - Affirmation: "I am building a strong, healthy body."
    - Action: Exercise + diet plan.
    - Result: Real transformation.

Key Insight

LOA is not supernatural. It's **focus psychology + consistent action.**

Summary

- LOA is a motivational framework, not a cosmic law.
- Real results = clarity + visualization + belief + action.
- The universe doesn't deliver — your focused brain and behavior do.

✦✦✦

PART 10

Neuroscience of Manifestation

Chapter 46 – How the Brain Creates Reality

When you "manifest" something, what's really happening? It starts in the **brain's perception system.**

Perception is Not Reality

- The brain doesn't see the world as it is — it filters and interprets it.
- Example: Two people in the same traffic jam.
    - One thinks: "This is ruining my day!" → stress rises.
    - Other thinks: "Great, I can listen to my audiobook." → calm mood.
- Same reality → different brain interpretation → different emotional outcomes.

Manifestation Link

When you focus on goals, your brain starts:

- Highlighting related opportunities.
- Ignoring distractions.
- Creating emotions that drive action.

👉 In short: your focus shapes your "personal reality."

Brain Science

The **prefrontal cortex** (decision-making center) directs attention.

- If you focus on negativity → it strengthens worry circuits.
- If you focus on goals → it strengthens solution-seeking circuits.

Summary

- Reality is filtered by the brain.

- Manifestation = shaping what the brain notices and prioritizes.
- Prefrontal cortex plays a key role.

✦✦✦

Chapter 47 – The Reticular Activating System (RAS)

The **RAS** is one of the most important brain networks for manifestation.

What is RAS?

- A bundle of nerves in the brainstem.
- Acts like a “filter” for information.
- Out of millions of signals per second, it decides what reaches your conscious mind.

Daily Life Examples

- You buy a red car → suddenly you notice red cars everywhere.
- You think about becoming a designer → you start noticing job ads, courses, or people in that field.

This isn't "the universe sending signs" — it's your **RAS spotlighting what matches your focus.**

Manifestation Application

- Write down your goals daily.
- Visualize them clearly.
- RAS will tune your brain to notice chances to move toward them.

Summary

- RAS filters reality based on focus.
- Explains why visualization and clarity make opportunities "appear."
- It's biology, not magic.

✦✦✦

Chapter 48 – Dopamine, Motivation, and Goal-Chasing

Manifestation also depends on the **dopamine system.**

What is Dopamine?

- A neurotransmitter often called the "motivation chemical."
- Released when you anticipate reward.
- Drives you to chase goals.

How Dopamine Affects Manifestation

- Clear goals + visualization → brain releases dopamine.

- Dopamine gives energy, focus, and persistence.
- Without dopamine, even simple goals feel impossible.

Example: Gym Training

- Person A says: “I’ll never get fit.” → low dopamine → no motivation.
- Person B visualizes: “I’m getting stronger each week.” → dopamine boosts → consistent training.

Practical Tip

Break big goals into **small wins.** Each win gives a dopamine hit, keeping motivation alive.

- Instead of “I’ll earn $10k/month,” start with: “This week I’ll make my first $100.”

Summary

- Dopamine drives motivation and persistence.

- Visualization and small wins trigger dopamine release.
- Essential for turning manifestation into consistent effort.

✦✦✦

Chapter 49 – Mirror Neurons and Visualization

Mirror neurons = special brain cells that fire both when you **do an action** and when you **imagine watching/doing it.**

Example: Sports Training

- Athletes visualizing perfect moves → activate same brain circuits as real practice.
- Studies show visualization improves performance almost as much as physical training.

Manifestation Connection

When you visualize:

- Speaking confidently.
- Running a successful business.
- Living a healthier lifestyle.

Your brain rehearses it as if it's already happening.

👉 This builds confidence and reduces fear of action.

Practical Exercise

Try **"mental rehearsal"** every night:

- Close eyes.
- Imagine your goal in detail (sight, sound, feeling).
- Repeat daily → your brain starts believing it's possible.

Summary

- Mirror neurons make visualization powerful.
- Brain "rehearses success" before real action.
- Builds confidence and reduces fear.

✦✦✦

Chapter 50 – Putting Neuroscience into Practice

Now let's connect all the brain systems into a **practical manifestation model.**

Step 1 – Clarity (Prefrontal Cortex)

Define clear goals → directs brain focus.

Step 2 – Spotlight (RAS)

Daily visualization → RAS highlights matching opportunities.

Step 3 – Motivation (Dopamine)

Break into small steps → dopamine keeps you moving.

Step 4 – Rehearsal (Mirror Neurons)

Visualize success → brain builds confidence and prepares.

Step 5 – Action + Adjustment

Act on opportunities → refine strategy as you go.

Case Study: Career Change

- Goal: Switch from job to freelancing.
- Prefrontal cortex: Writes down exact freelancing niche.
- RAS: Notices ads, events, people in freelancing.
- Dopamine: Feels motivated after each small client project.
- Mirror neurons: Visualizes pitching confidently → does it in real life.
- Outcome: Gradual but real career shift.

Summary

- Neuroscience explains manifestation through brain systems.

- Prefrontal cortex, RAS, dopamine, and mirror neurons all play roles.
- Manifestation works when brain focus + action combine.

✦✦✦

PART 11

Common Myths & Misconceptions

Chapter 51 – Myth 1: “Manifestation is Instant”

One of the biggest lies in the self-help world is:

👉 *“Just think about it and it will happen overnight.”*

Why People Believe This

- Social media “gurus” show fake success stories.
- The human brain craves **quick fixes.**
- Movies like *The Secret* popularized “ask and receive instantly.”

The Reality

Manifestation is not instant.

- Your brain doesn't work like a 24-hour delivery service.
- It takes **time, repetition, and consistent action** for neural rewiring.
- Big life changes = months or years of effort.

Example

- Instant myth: "I visualized money, and tomorrow I'll get $10,000."
- Reality: "I visualized building financial skills, worked for 6 months, and opportunities opened."

Summary

- Instant manifestation = myth.
- Real results = long-term effort + persistence.

✦✦✦

Chapter 52 – Myth 2: "You Attract Only What You Think"

LOA often says: *"If you think negative, you'll attract negative."*

The Problem With This Belief

- Creates guilt: People blame themselves for bad events ("I must have thought wrong").
- Oversimplifies reality: Accidents, illnesses, or hardships happen regardless of thoughts.
- Can be cruel: Telling someone with cancer they "manifested it" is harmful.

The Reality

- Thoughts influence behavior, not external random events.
- Positive mindset helps you act better in situations.
- But you cannot "think away" natural disasters or diseases.

Balanced View

- You don't control everything.
- But you control **your focus, response, and habits.**

👉 That's where manifestation really works.

Summary

- Negative thinking doesn't cause every problem.
- You can't control all events, only your response.
- Manifestation is about mindset + action, not blaming yourself.

Shweta Jaiswal

✦✦✦

Chapter 53 – Myth 3: "Vision Boards Alone Will Change Your Life"

Vision boards = posters with pictures of your dream house, car, job, etc.
Many coaches claim: *"Just look at it daily, and it will come true."*

Why It Feels Good

- Looking at pictures releases dopamine.
- Gives temporary motivation.
- Feels like progress without actual effort.

The Reality

Vision boards are helpful **only if paired with action.**

- They remind your brain of your goals.
- But without steps → nothing happens.

Example

- Person A: Makes a vision board of a fit body → but eats junk daily. → No results.
- Person B: Makes vision board → uses it as motivation to join gym + eat better. → Real results.

Summary

- Vision boards are tools, not magic.
- Useful for reminders, but action creates change.

✦✦✦

Chapter 54 – Myth 4: "Manifestation Replaces Hard Work"

Many people misunderstand manifestation as:

👉 *"I don't need to work hard, the universe will do it for me."*

The Problem

- Creates laziness.
- Stops people from developing skills.
- Leads to disappointment when nothing changes.

The Reality

Manifestation **fuels** hard work — it doesn't replace it.

- Visualization builds belief.
- Affirmations strengthen persistence.
- But only consistent effort = results.

Example: Learning a Language

- Myth: Repeat "I'm fluent in Spanish" → magically speak it.
- Reality: Affirmation + daily practice + classes → fluency.

Summary

- Hard work is non-negotiable.
- Manifestation is a mental support system, not a replacement for effort.

✦✦✦

Chapter 55 – Myth 5: "The Universe is Your Genie"

Some LOA teachers say:

👉 *"The universe is listening. Just order like Amazon, and it delivers."*

Why It's Dangerous

- Makes people passive.
- Creates magical thinking.
- When goals fail → people feel betrayed by the universe.

The Reality

- The "universe" is a metaphor.
- It's really your **brain, habits, and environment** working together.
- Instead of waiting, you must create your results.

Balanced Perspective

- Use "the universe" as poetic language.
- But don't expect magic.
- Manifestation = clarity + focus + resilience.

Summary

- The universe isn't your genie.
- Results come from your brain, not magic delivery.
- Manifestation works through natural psychology.

✦✦✦

PART 12

Real-Life Case Studies & Experiments

Chapter 56 – Case Study: Athletes and Visualization

One of the strongest proofs for manifestation techniques comes from **sports science.**

The Experiment

- In the 1980s, Russian sports scientists studied Olympic athletes.
- They divided them into 4 groups:
    1. 100% physical training.
    2. 75% physical + 25% mental rehearsal.
    3. 50% physical + 50% mental rehearsal.
    4. 25% physical + 75% mental rehearsal.

👉 Surprisingly, **Group 3 (50/50)** performed the best in competition.

Why?

- Visualization activated the same neural pathways as real practice.
- This boosted **confidence, precision, and readiness.**

Lesson

Visualization is not magic — it's mental training.

- Athletes use it daily to improve performance.
- Works best when paired with real effort.

Summary

- Athletes proved manifestation (visualization) helps.
- Works by rehearsing the brain, not by cosmic attraction.
- Best results = balance of mental + physical practice.

✦✦✦

Chapter 57 – Case Study: Students and Exam Performance

Can affirmations and manifestation improve academic success?

The Experiment

- A psychology study tested two groups of students before exams:
  - Group A: Visualized getting good grades and felt confident.
  - Group B: Visualized the **process** — studying daily, focusing, completing tasks.

👉 Group B scored significantly higher.

Why?

- Visualizing the outcome (grades) gave false confidence.
- Visualizing the process created better **study habits and motivation.**

Lesson

Outcome-based manifestation = weak.

Process-based manifestation = strong.

Summary

- Students proved process visualization beats outcome visualization.
- Manifestation is most powerful when focused on **steps, not just dreams.**

✦✦✦

Chapter 58 – Experiment: The Placebo Effect

One of the most fascinating scientific proofs of belief is the **placebo effect.**

What is Placebo?

- When patients believe they're receiving real medicine (but get sugar pills), they often show real improvement.
- The brain releases endorphins and activates healing pathways **just because of belief.**

Manifestation Connection

Affirmations and visualization work the same way:

- Belief changes brain chemistry.
- This leads to **better mood, focus, and resilience.**

Example

- Placebo knee surgeries: Patients who only *thought* they had surgery (but didn't) improved almost as much as real patients.

Lesson

Belief itself is medicine.
Manifestation harnesses this same brain mechanism.

✅ Chapter Summary

- Placebo proves belief changes reality (through the brain).
- Manifestation is a structured placebo — belief + action = results.

✦✦✦

Chapter 59 – Case Study: Entrepreneurs Using LOA

Many entrepreneurs credit manifestation for success — but not in the "magic genie" way.

Example: Sara Blakely (Founder of Spanx)

- Visualized herself running a successful company before she even had a product.
- Repeated affirmations to boost her self-confidence.
- Took bold actions, like pitching investors despite rejection.
- Outcome: Became the youngest self-made female billionaire.

Analysis

- Visualization gave confidence.
- Affirmations killed self-doubt.
- Action turned dreams into reality.

Lesson

Entrepreneurs don't sit waiting. They **use manifestation to fuel courage and persistence.**

Summary

- Entrepreneurs like Sara Blakely use LOA as motivation, not magic.
- Manifestation = clarity + courage + relentless action.

✦✦✦

Chapter 60 – Experiment: Gratitude Journaling and Happiness

Gratitude is a form of affirmation — focusing on positive aspects of life.

The Experiment

- Researchers asked 3 groups of people to journal for 10 weeks:
    - Group A: Wrote 5 things they were grateful for.
    - Group B: Wrote 5 irritations or complaints.
    - Group C: Wrote neutral events.

👉 Group A reported:

- More optimism.
- Better sleep.
- Fewer doctor visits.
- Higher happiness levels.

Why?

- Gratitude rewires brain circuits toward positivity.
- Increases dopamine and serotonin.
- Reduces stress hormones.

Lesson

Simple affirmations like "I am grateful" shift mental health dramatically.

Summary

- Gratitude experiments prove manifestation boosts happiness.

- Affirmations can rewire mood and health.
- Focus on positive reality creates real change.

✦✦✦

PART 13

Dangers, Misuse, and Toxic Positivity

Chapter 61 – The Risk of False Hope

Manifestation can be powerful — but it can also create **false hope** if misunderstood.

What is False Hope?

When people believe manifestation = magic, they:

- Wait for results without action.
- Expect instant success.
- Get crushed when nothing happens.

Example

- A jobless person repeats: "I'm rich, I'm rich," but never applies for jobs or builds skills.
- Months later → no money → disappointment → loss of faith.

The Problem

False hope = false expectations.

- Leads to **frustration, self-doubt, and depression.**
- Some even quit trying after failure.

The Fix

- Balance belief with reality.
- Use manifestation as motivation, not as guarantee.
- Remember: **effort = bridge between dreams and reality.**

✅ **Chapter Summary**

- Misuse creates false hope.

- Leads to disappointment if not paired with action.
- Manifestation must be realistic.

✦✦✦

Chapter 62 – Self-Blame and Guilt Trap

Another danger is when people blame themselves for every bad thing, thinking they "manifested" it.

How This Happens

- LOA often says: "You attract everything."
- People then assume:
  - Illness? → My fault.
  - Car accident? → My negative thoughts.
  - Loss of job? → I must have manifested it.

Why It's Harmful

- Creates **toxic guilt and shame.**
- Stops people from seeking real solutions (medical help, financial planning, therapy).
- Feels like punishment instead of empowerment.

The Reality

- You cannot control everything.
- Life has randomness, luck, and external factors.
- You are responsible only for **your choices and actions.**

Balanced View

- Don't blame yourself for every negative event.
- Focus on what you can control → attitude, learning, resilience.

Summary

- Self-blame = dangerous misuse.

- You don't manifest every bad event.
- Manifestation is about empowerment, not guilt.

✦✦✦

Chapter 63 – Toxic Positivity

Sometimes manifestation culture promotes **"be positive no matter what."**

👉 This is called **toxic positivity.**

What is Toxic Positivity?

- Forcing happiness even when you feel sad.
- Denying real emotions (anger, grief, stress).
- Pretending everything is perfect.

Why It's Dangerous

- Suppressing emotions increases anxiety and depression.

- Makes people feel invalidated ("I shouldn't feel sad").
- Blocks real healing.

Example

- Person loses a loved one. Friends say: "Don't cry, stay positive, manifest happiness."
- Instead of grieving naturally, the person feels **guilty for being sad.**

The Reality

Healthy positivity = hope + resilience.
Toxic positivity = denial of real feelings.

Balanced Practice

- Allow yourself to feel pain.
- Use affirmations like:
    - "It's okay to feel sad. I will heal."
    - "I am strong enough to go through this."

Summary

- Toxic positivity = denying real emotions.
- Healthy manifestation = balance of honesty + hope.

✦✦✦

Chapter 64 – Escaping Reality vs. Facing It

Manifestation can sometimes become an **escape mechanism.**

The Problem

- People spend hours visualizing instead of acting.
- They use affirmations as fantasy instead of tools.
- Reality is ignored.

Example

- A student keeps visualizing "I'm a topper" but never studies.

- Reality: fails exam → blames manifestation.

The Danger

Escaping reality prevents growth.

- Manifestation becomes daydreaming.
- No real progress happens.

The Fix

- Use manifestation as a **launchpad** for action.
- Spend 5 minutes visualizing, then spend hours working.

Summary

- Don’t escape into manifestation.
- Use it to face reality with more strength.

✦✦✦

Chapter 65 – Manipulation and Fake Gurus

Unfortunately, many "manifestation coaches" exploit people's hopes.

The Problem

- Gurus sell false promises:
  - "Manifest $10,000 in 7 days."
  - "Buy my $999 course and the universe will bless you."
- Vulnerable people fall into traps.

How They Manipulate

- Use testimonials (often fake).
- Show luxury lifestyles to appear "manifested."
- Blame failure on the student ("You didn't believe enough").

The Reality

- True manifestation is free — it's a mental practice.
- You don't need expensive rituals or courses.
- Real growth comes from consistent practice + self-discipline.

How to Protect Yourself

- Question: Is this advice backed by science?
- Check: Does it encourage real action, or just waiting?
- Avoid: Anyone who promises "instant money" or "secret cosmic codes."

Summary

- Fake gurus exploit manifestation myths.
- Real manifestation doesn't require buying anything.
- Protect yourself by staying scientific and practical.

✦✦✦

PART 14

Tools & Techniques That Actually Work

Chapter 66 – Journaling for Clarity

One of the simplest yet most powerful manifestation tools is **journaling.**

Why Journaling Works

- Writing forces clarity → vague thoughts become concrete.
- Activates both left (logic) and right (creativity) brain.
- Creates a personal record → you track growth over time.

Methods of Journaling

1. **Goal Journaling**
    - Write your top 3 goals daily.
    - Example: "I am working toward building my business."
2. **Affirmation Journaling**
    - Write affirmations in the present tense.
    - Example: "I am confident in every meeting I attend."
3. **Gratitude Journaling**
    - Each night, write 3 things you're grateful for.
    - Example: "I'm grateful for my supportive family."

Example in Action

- Student journals:
    - Goal: "I will improve my grades."

- Affirmation: "I am disciplined with my study schedule."
- Gratitude: "I'm thankful for the resources I have."

- Result: More focus + less stress.

Summary

- Journaling brings clarity and direction.
- Combine goals, affirmations, and gratitude for maximum effect.

✦✦✦

Chapter 67 – Visualization Techniques

Visualization is one of the most researched and powerful manifestation tools.

How to Do It

1. **Relax First** – Close eyes, breathe deeply.
2. **Create a Mental Movie** – Imagine yourself achieving the goal.
3. **Engage the Senses** – What do you see, hear, feel, smell?
4. **Add Emotion** – Feel the excitement of success.

Types of Visualization

- **Outcome Visualization** → Imagine the end result (graduation day, dream house).
- **Process Visualization** → Imagine the steps (studying, practicing, networking).

👉 Science shows **process visualization** works better for performance.

Example

- Athlete visualizes running the perfect race.
- Brain fires neurons as if actually running.
- Performance improves in real training.

Summary

- Visualization rewires the brain.
- Best results = combining outcome + process visualization.

✦✦✦

Chapter 68 – Affirmation Crafting

Affirmations are powerful — but only when done correctly.

Rules of Effective Affirmations

1. **Present Tense**
    - Wrong: "I will be confident."
    - Right: "I am confident."
2. **Positive Language**
    - Wrong: "I am not nervous."
    - Right: "I am calm and prepared."
3. **Specificity**

  - Vague: "I am successful."
  - Specific: "I am building a successful online business."

Daily Practice

- Speak affirmations aloud.
- Write them down 5–10 times.
- Record and listen to them daily.

Example Affirmations

- "I handle challenges with confidence."
- "I take consistent action toward my goals."
- "I deserve success and happiness."

Summary

- Affirmations must be present, positive, and specific.
- Daily repetition wires beliefs into the subconscious.

Shweta Jaiswal

✦✦✦

Chapter 69 – Gratitude Practices

Gratitude is a simple but life-changing technique.

Why Gratitude Works

- Shifts focus from what's missing → to what's present.
- Boosts serotonin and dopamine (happiness chemicals).
- Reduces stress hormones (cortisol).

Practical Gratitude Methods

1. **Morning Gratitude Ritual**

   - Before checking phone, list 3 things you're thankful for.

2. **Gratitude Letters**
   - Write a thank-you letter to someone (even if you don't send it).

3. **Gratitude Walks**
   - During a walk, mentally list everything you appreciate.

Example

- Worker feeling stressed starts writing 3 gratitude points daily.
- Within weeks → reports better sleep, optimism, and energy.

Summary

- Gratitude rewires your brain to see abundance.
- Daily practice builds resilience and happiness.

✦✦✦

Chapter 70 – Meditation and Mindfulness

The foundation of manifestation success is **mental stillness.**

Why Meditation Helps

- Quiet mind → clearer focus on goals.
- Reduces stress → better decision making.
- Strengthens awareness → you notice opportunities faster.

Techniques for Beginners

1. **Breathing Meditation**

   - Focus on deep breaths for 5–10 minutes.

2. **Mindfulness Meditation**
   - Pay attention to present moment (sounds, sensations).

3. **Guided Visualization Meditation**
   - Listen to an audio guide that blends relaxation + manifestation.

Example

- Busy entrepreneur practices 10 minutes of meditation daily.
- Reports improved focus, calmer mindset, and faster progress on goals.

Summary

- Meditation clears the mental noise.
- Increases focus, calmness, and goal alignment.
- Essential foundation for manifestation success.

Shweta Jaiswal

✦✦✦

PART 15

Daily Habits for Long-Term Success

Chapter 71 – Morning Rituals

How you start your morning sets the tone for your entire day.

Why Morning Rituals Matter

- Brain is most **impressionable** in the first hour (theta brainwaves).
- Morning routines strengthen discipline and consistency.
- Positive start = higher productivity all day.

Practical Morning Habits

1. **Affirmations** – Speak or write 3–5 empowering statements.
2. **Visualization** – Spend 2 minutes imagining your top goal.
3. **Gratitude** – Write 3 things you're thankful for.
4. **Movement** – Stretching, yoga, or a short workout.
5. **Silence** – 5 minutes of meditation or deep breathing.

Example

- Entrepreneur starts day with:
    - Affirmation: "I am confident in my meetings today."
    - Gratitude: "I'm thankful for supportive clients."
    - 5 minutes meditation.
- Reports calmer, sharper decision-making throughout the day.

Summary

- Morning rituals = strong foundation for manifestation.
- Small consistent actions create long-term mental rewiring.

✦✦✦

Chapter 72 – Nighttime Routines

Evenings are as powerful as mornings for manifestation.

Why Night Routines Work

- Last thoughts before sleep enter subconscious.
- Brain processes them during dreaming (memory consolidation).
- Night rituals reduce stress and improve sleep quality.

Practical Night Habits

1. **Gratitude Journaling** – List 3 wins or blessings of the day.
2. **Affirmation Review** – Repeat affirmations before bed.
3. **Visualization** – Imagine tomorrow going smoothly.
4. **Digital Detox** – Avoid screens 30–60 mins before sleep.

Example

- Student visualizes the next day's exam prep before bed.
- Sleeps calmly, wakes up focused.
- Performs better compared to nights of anxious scrolling.

Summary

- Night routines program the subconscious.
- Use them to reduce stress and create tomorrow's success.

✦✦✦

Chapter 73 – The Power of Small Wins

Manifestation is often misunderstood as chasing only **big goals.** But the secret lies in **celebrating small wins daily.**

Why Small Wins Matter

- Boost dopamine → keeps motivation alive.
- Builds confidence step by step.
- Prevents overwhelm from massive goals.

Examples of Small Wins

- Finishing 30 minutes of study.
- Saying “no” to junk food.

- Sending one job application.

How to Track Small Wins

- Keep a "Victory Log" notebook.
- Each day, write 1–3 small wins.
- Review weekly → see proof of growth.

Example in Action

- Overweight person logs:
  - Day 1: Walked 10 minutes.
  - Day 5: Walked 20 minutes.
  - Day 15: Jogged 30 minutes.
- Motivation grows → full lifestyle change.

Summary

- Small wins build momentum.
- Tracking them strengthens belief in manifestation.

✦✦✦

Chapter 74 – Consistency Over Intensity

One of the biggest mistakes people make = trying to do too much too fast.

Why Consistency Wins

- Habits stick better when repeated daily in small doses.
- Intensity leads to burnout → quitting.
- The subconscious responds better to repetition than to rare effort.

Example

- Affirmations: Better to do 2 minutes daily than 1 hour once a week.
- Exercise: Better to walk 15 mins daily than run 5 km once a month.

Science Behind It

- Neural pathways strengthen through **frequency, not intensity.**
- Small actions repeated = brain automation.

Practical Tip

- Choose "non-negotiables" → 3–5 small daily habits.
- Even if life gets busy, never skip them.

Summary

- Consistency > intensity for long-term success.
- Small daily habits = strongest manifestation tool.

Shweta Jaiswal

✦✦✦

Chapter 75 – Habit Stacking

Habit stacking is a smart method to make manifestation automatic.

What is Habit Stacking?

- Linking a new habit to an existing one.
- Example: "After I brush my teeth, I'll say my affirmations."

Why It Works

- Uses old routines as reminders.

- Builds habits without needing willpower.

Examples of Habit Stacking

- After drinking morning tea → write 3 gratitude points.
- After opening laptop → read one affirmation card.
- After turning off alarm → visualize your top goal.

Case Example

- Busy mother stacks affirmations with school drop-off.
- Every drive → repeats 3 empowering statements.
- Builds confidence without adding "extra time."

Summary

- Habit stacking makes manifestation effortless.
- Piggyback new habits onto existing ones.
- Turns rituals into automatic lifestyle.

✦✦✦

PART 16

Manifestation and Relationships

Chapter 76 – Self-Love Comes First

Before manifesting healthy relationships, you must first build **self-love.**

Why Self-Love Matters

- You attract what you believe you deserve.
- Without self-love, you tolerate disrespect or toxicity.
- Confidence radiates outward → influences how others treat you.

Practical Self-Love Habits

1. **Mirror Affirmations** – Look into a mirror daily and say:
    - "I am worthy of love and respect."
    - "I am enough as I am."
2. **Boundaries** – Practice saying "no" without guilt.
3. **Celebrate Yourself** – Note daily wins, even small ones.

Example

- A woman lacking confidence repeated: "I am lovable and valuable" daily.
- Over weeks → self-worth grew → she stopped tolerating toxic friends.
- Eventually, she built healthier connections.

Summary

- Self-love is the foundation of all manifestation in relationships.
- Without it, even affirmations for others won't work.

✦✦✦

Chapter 77 – Attracting Healthy Friendships

Friends shape your mindset more than you realize.

Why Friendships Matter

- Research: Your habits and happiness mirror your closest circle.
- Positive friends encourage growth → negative ones pull you down.

How to Manifest Better Friendships

1. **Clarity** – Write qualities you want in friends (loyal, positive, ambitious).

2. **Visualization** – Imagine spending joyful time with such friends.
3. **Affirmations** – "I attract friendships that uplift me."
4. **Action** – Join groups, events, or communities aligned with your values.

Example

- A man tired of gossip-based friendships affirmed: "I deserve supportive, inspiring friends."
- He joined a fitness group → built genuine bonds → friendships aligned with his goals.

Summary

- Friendships can be manifested by clarity + action.
- Right circle = faster personal growth.

✦✦✦

Chapter 78 – Love and Romantic Relationships

Many people use manifestation to attract love — but it must be grounded in reality.

The Misuse

- People think: "If I visualize, my crush will magically love me."
- ❌ Wrong → that's manipulation, not manifestation.

The Right Way

Manifestation for love = **becoming the partner you want to attract.**

- Want respect? → Be respectful.
- Want trust? → Be trustworthy.
- Want loyalty? → Be loyal yourself.

Affirmations for Love

- "I am ready for a loving, healthy relationship."
- "I attract a partner who values me for who I am."

Example

- A man kept affirming: "I am lovable and confident."
- He worked on self-growth → improved social confidence.
- Naturally attracted a partner aligned with his energy.

Summary

- Love manifestation = self-growth first.
- Focus on alignment, not forcing specific people.

✦✦✦

Chapter 79 – Healing Toxic Relationships

Manifestation can also help heal or exit toxic bonds.

Recognizing Toxicity

- Constant disrespect.
- Lack of trust.
- Energy drain instead of energy boost.

How Manifestation Helps

1. **Clarity** – Write what's unacceptable.
2. **Affirmation** – "I deserve relationships that respect me."

3. **Action** – Set boundaries or walk away if needed.
4. **Healing** – Use affirmations like: "I forgive myself for staying too long, I choose peace now."

Example

- A woman in a controlling relationship affirmed daily: "I am strong and free."
- This built courage → she set boundaries → eventually left and rebuilt her life.

Summary

- Manifestation isn't about fixing toxic people.
- It's about strengthening yourself to choose better relationships.

✦✦✦

Chapter 80 – Communication and Energy Exchange

Relationships thrive or break based on **communication.**

Why Communication = Energy

- Words carry frequency → affirmations apply in conversations too.
- Positive language attracts openness.
- Negative language creates walls.

Manifestation in Communication

1. **Before conversations**, affirm:
    - "I speak with clarity and calmness."

    - “I listen to understand, not to react.”

2. **Visualization** – Imagine the talk going respectfully.
3. **Gratitude in Relationships** – Regularly express appreciation.

Example

- A manager affirmed before meetings: “I communicate with clarity.”
- Result: Less conflict, smoother teamwork, stronger respect.

Summary

- Relationships = daily energy exchange.
- Manifestation works by aligning communication with respect and gratitude.

✦✦✦

PART 17

Success Stories and Case Studies

Chapter 81 – From Fear to Confidence: A Student's Story

Background

Ravi, a 19-year-old engineering student, struggled with public speaking. He avoided presentations, feared classroom participation, and believed he was "just bad at speaking."

The Turning Point

One of his professors introduced him to affirmations and visualization. Ravi decided to test it for a semester.

- Daily Affirmation: *"I speak with clarity and confidence."*

- Visualization: Before sleep, imagined delivering a smooth presentation.
- Small Action: Practiced speaking to a mirror for 5 minutes daily.

The Result

At first, no miracle happened — nerves were still there. But after 6 weeks:

- He volunteered for a small classroom presentation.
- His confidence improved slowly with each attempt.
- By semester's end, he was chosen to present a group project in front of 100 students.

Lesson

Manifestation didn't erase fear overnight — it rewired his mindset so he took consistent action. That combination = real growth.

Takeaway: Affirmations + visualization + small steps = transformation.

✦✦✦

Chapter 82 – Entrepreneur Manifesting Business Growth

Background

Meera, 28, wanted to grow her online clothing business. Sales were stagnant, and she often thought: *"Maybe I'm not cut out for this."*

The Shift

She discovered manifestation through journaling and gratitude.

- Each morning she journaled: *"I run a growing and profitable business."*
- She kept a gratitude log: *"I'm thankful for each customer."*

- Visualization: imagined her shop receiving more orders daily.

Action Steps

- She started posting consistently on Instagram.
- Responded politely and personally to customers.
- Introduced small discounts and referral bonuses.

The Result

- Within 3 months → sales grew by 40%.
- Customers left more positive reviews.
- She attracted collaborations with influencers.

Lesson

Manifestation didn't magically bring sales. It boosted her **focus, energy, and action** — which brought real growth.

Takeaway: Gratitude + visualization fuels confidence → which fuels smarter work.

✦✦✦

Chapter 83 – Healing After a Breakup

Background

Arjun went through a painful breakup. His self-esteem collapsed, and he repeated in his mind: *"I'll never find love again."*

The Shift

He decided to use affirmations not for a partner, but for **self-healing.**

- Daily Affirmation: *"I am whole and worthy on my own."*

- Visualization: imagined a peaceful, happy version of himself.
- Gratitude: focused on family and friends who supported him.

Action Steps

- Started journaling emotions instead of bottling them up.
- Took up gym workouts as a form of self-care.
- Stopped chasing his ex and redirected energy toward self-growth.

The Result

- Within months, he regained confidence.
- Friends noticed his energy shift.
- A year later, he naturally attracted a healthier, more aligned relationship.

Lesson

Manifestation isn't about forcing love — it's about **healing yourself first.** When you align internally, the right partner comes naturally.

Takeaway: Healing affirmations build strength for healthier relationships.

✦✦✦

Chapter 84 – Career Growth Through Affirmations

Background

Priya, 32, worked as a mid-level manager. She felt stuck, underpaid, and invisible in her company.

The Shift

She began using affirmations around confidence and value:

- *"I deserve recognition for my contributions."*
- *"I lead with clarity and confidence."*

She also visualized herself leading meetings and negotiating her salary.

Action Steps

- Prepared thoroughly before meetings.
- Started speaking up with new ideas.
- Booked a session with a career coach for negotiation tips.

The Result

- Within 6 months, her confidence was noticeable.
- Boss gave her a chance to lead a project.
- Later, she negotiated a 20% salary raise.

Lesson

Affirmations didn't *cause* the raise. But they rewired her confidence → which influenced her actions → which got her results.

Takeaway: Manifestation upgrades mindset, which upgrades performance.

✦✦✦

Chapter 85 – When Manifestation Fails: A Cautionary Tale

Background

Sahil read about manifestation online and believed all he needed was to "think rich." He repeated affirmations like: *"I am a millionaire"* — but took no action.

The Result

- No change in income.
- Grew frustrated, saying "Manifestation is fake."
- Stopped trying after a few weeks.

The Real Issue

- Affirmations were unrealistic (jumping from low income to millionaire instantly).
- No aligned actions (skills, networking, effort).
- Expecting miracles without work.

Lesson

Manifestation fails when used as **wishful thinking** instead of mindset training.

Takeaway: Manifestation is the spark, **action is the fire.** Both are needed.

✦✦✦

PART 18

Busting Popular Myths About Manifestation

Chapter 86 – Myth: "Manifestation is Magic"

The Belief

Many think manifestation = magic. That if you just write "I want 1 crore" in a diary, it will appear.

The Reality

- Science shows manifestation is a **mental tool**, not supernatural.
- Affirmations and visualization work by reprogramming your **subconscious mind**, not bending reality like magic.
- Without action, affirmations remain empty words.

Example

- Person A: Writes "I want to be rich" daily but does nothing → no change.
- Person B: Writes "I'm improving my finances," studies investing, applies for better jobs → real improvement.

☑ **Truth:** Manifestation is psychology, not magic.

✦✦✦

Chapter 87 – Myth: "Just Think Positive and Everything Will Happen"

The Belief

The law of attraction is often sold as: "If you only think positive thoughts, you'll get everything you want."

The Reality

- Positive thinking helps, but it's not enough.
- Success = mindset + skills + action + persistence.
- Ignoring reality and forcing fake positivity can be toxic.

Science Proof

- Studies show optimism improves resilience.
- But outcomes depend on **effort + strategy**, not thoughts alone.

Example

- A student can't just "think positive" about exams.
- They must study → positivity helps reduce anxiety, but preparation brings results.

✅ **Truth:** Positive thinking helps focus, but doesn't replace effort.

✦✦✦

Chapter 88 – Myth: "You Can Attract Anyone You Want"

The Belief

Some claim you can "manifest" a specific person to fall in love with you.

The Reality

- You cannot control another person's free will.
- Forcing someone's love is manipulation, not manifestation.
- True manifestation works by aligning **your energy** → which attracts compatible partners naturally.

Example

- Wrong Way: Repeating "My crush will text me today."
- Right Way: Affirming "I am lovable and attract healthy relationships."
- Result: Instead of chasing one person, you grow and meet someone aligned.

☑ **Truth:** You can attract love, but not force someone's feelings.

✦✦✦

Chapter 89 – Myth: "Manifestation Works Overnight"

The Belief

People want quick results: "Say affirmations tonight, see results tomorrow."

The Reality

- Manifestation takes time → because it's about **building habits and rewiring the subconscious.**
- The brain learns through repetition → usually weeks or months, not days.
- Speed depends on the size of the goal and consistency of effort.

Science Proof

- Neural rewiring (neuroplasticity) usually takes 21–66 days of repetition.

Example

- If you want confidence, repeating affirmations once won't work.
- Daily repetition + practice over 2–3 months = visible change.

✅ **Truth:** Manifestation is a marathon, not a sprint.

✦✦✦

Chapter 90 – Myth: "Manifestation is Just Fake/Delusion"

The Belief

Skeptics say: "Manifestation is just delusion, daydreaming, or nonsense."

The Reality

- Manifestation isn't delusion if practiced realistically.
- It uses proven psychology:
    - **Reticular Activating System (RAS):** Brain filters what you focus on.

- **Placebo Effect:** Belief can trigger real physical changes.
- **Self-Fulfilling Prophecy:** Expectations influence behavior.

Example

- A job seeker who believes "I won't get hired" → low energy in interviews → rejection.
- A job seeker who affirms "I am capable" → shows confidence → higher chance of success.

✅ **Truth:** Manifestation is real psychology, not fantasy — as long as you combine it with action.

✦✦✦

PART 19

Building a Personal Manifestation System

Chapter 91 – Step 1: Clarity of Goals

Why Clarity Matters

- A vague goal = vague results.
- The brain needs **specific instructions** to filter reality through the Reticular Activating System (RAS).

👉 Saying *"I want success"* is too vague.

👉 Saying *"I want to become a published author in the next 12 months"* gives direction.

How to Get Clarity

1. Write 3–5 top goals for the next year.

2. For each, ask:
    - *What exactly do I want?*
    - *Why do I want it?*
    - *When do I want it by?*

Exercise: Goal-Setting Journal

- Write one clear statement:
  "By December 2025, I am earning ₹80,000 monthly through my graphic design freelancing business."

Key Lesson: A clear, measurable goal is the foundation of manifestation.

✦✦✦

Chapter 92 – Step 2: Designing Affirmations That Work

Why Normal Affirmations Fail

- People repeat unrealistic ones like *"I am a billionaire"* when they're broke.
- Subconscious rejects them → feels fake → no change.

Formula for Effective Affirmations

1. Present tense: *"I am improving..."*
2. Positive language: Avoid "not" or "never."
3. Believable yet challenging.

Examples

❌ Wrong: "I am a billionaire right now."

✅ Right: "I am learning the skills to increase my income every month."

❌ Wrong: "I will never be lonely."

✅ Right: "I am attracting supportive, loving relationships."

Daily Practice

- 5 affirmations repeated morning & night.
- Write them down, say them aloud, and visualize them.

Key Lesson: Affirmations must be realistic enough to feel true, yet inspiring enough to push growth.

✦✦✦

Chapter 93 – Step 3: Visualization Practice

Why Visualization Works

- Brain often doesn't distinguish between imagination and reality.
- Athletes use visualization to improve performance.
- Builds **neural pathways** before the actual event.

How to Visualize Effectively

1. **Quiet space** – close your eyes, breathe deeply.
2. **Detailed imagery** – imagine sights, sounds, emotions.
3. **Feel it** – not just seeing, but *experiencing*.

Example

- If your goal = public speaking, visualize:
    - Standing on stage.
    - Audience clapping.
    - Your voice calm and clear.

Practice Tip

- 5 minutes morning, 5 minutes before sleep.

Key Lesson: Visualization creates a "mental rehearsal" that prepares the brain for success.

✦✦✦

Chapter 94 – Step 4: Daily Action Plan

Why Action = The Missing Link

- Without action, manifestation is daydreaming.
- Daily action = proof to the subconscious that you are serious.

System for Daily Action

1. Write one small step toward your goal daily.
   - Want fitness? → 15 min walk today.
   - Want money? → Apply for 2 jobs today.
   - Want confidence? → Talk to one stranger today.
2. Track progress in a "Manifestation Journal."

3. Review weekly.

Example

If your goal is to start a YouTube channel:

- Day 1: Write 10 video ideas.
- Day 2: Record 30-sec practice video.
- Day 3: Learn basic editing.

Key Lesson: Manifestation works only when combined with **consistent daily actions.**

✦✦✦

Chapter 95 – Step 5: Tracking and Adjusting

Why Tracking Matters

- Without review, you don't know what's working.
- Tracking = builds self-accountability.

How to Track

1. Weekly reflection:
    - *What actions did I take?*
    - *What results came?*
2. Adjust affirmations if they feel fake or stale.

3. Adjust visualization if it no longer excites you.

Example of Adjustment

- Initial affirmation: *"I earn ₹80,000/month freelancing."*
- If results are slow, adjust to: *"I am gaining new clients monthly and steadily increasing my income."*

Tool: Manifestation Journal Layout

- Date
- Goal of the week
- Affirmations used
- Actions taken
- Wins + Challenges
- Next steps

Key Lesson: Manifestation is not rigid. Review + adjust keeps your system alive.

✦✦✦

PART 20

Living a Manifestation Lifestyle & Conclusion

Chapter 96 – Manifestation as a Daily Habit

Why Habits Matter

Manifestation isn't something you do once and forget. It's like brushing your teeth — small daily actions that keep your mind "clean" and aligned.

👉 If you stop brushing for weeks, your teeth suffer.

👉 If you stop affirming, visualizing, and acting, your mindset slips back to old patterns.

Daily Habit Checklist

1. **Morning Affirmations** – 5 statements.
2. **5-Minute Visualization** – feel your goal as real.
3. **Gratitude Note** – 3 things you're thankful for.

4. **One Small Action** – something aligned with your goal.

☑ **Lesson:** Make manifestation part of your morning/evening routine.

✦✦✦

Chapter 97 – Handling Doubts and Failures

The Reality

Even with manifestation, life will test you. Failures happen. Doubts creep in.

👉 The difference? Manifestors use setbacks as **fuel** instead of quitting.

How to Handle Doubts

1. Accept them: "It's normal to feel doubt."
2. Counter with gentle affirmations: *"Even if I fail, I learn and grow."*
3. Reframe failure as feedback: "What is this teaching me?"

Example

- Student fails one exam.

  ❌ Old mindset: "I'm useless."

  ✅ Manifestation mindset: "This shows I need new study methods. I can still improve."

✅ **Lesson:** Manifestation doesn't erase failure, it changes how you respond.

✦✦✦

Chapter 98 – Combining Manifestation with Practical Skills

The Trap

Some people only do affirmations, expecting results.

Others ignore mindset, focusing only on hard skills.

👉 The secret is **balance.**

Formula for Success

Mindset + Skills + Action = Results

- Mindset → belief you *can* do it.
- Skills → actual tools to perform.
- Action → applying both consistently.

Example

- Want to become a YouTuber?
  - Mindset: “My content is valuable.”
  - Skills: Learn editing, storytelling, SEO.
  - Action: Post weekly videos.

✅ **Lesson:** Manifestation is the accelerator. Skills and action are the car.

✦✦✦

Chapter 99 – Living in Alignment

What is Alignment?

Alignment means your **thoughts, words, and actions** match your goals.

👉 If you affirm "I'm healthy" but eat junk food daily, that's misalignment.
👉 If you affirm "I'm confident" but avoid every challenge, that's misalignment.

How to Live Aligned

1. Ask daily: *"Does this action match my goals?"*
2. Drop habits that pull you backward.

3. Surround yourself with people who support your growth.

Example

Goal = financial freedom.

- Misaligned: Spending on unnecessary luxuries daily.
- Aligned: Saving, investing, learning money management.

✅ **Lesson:** Alignment makes manifestation faster and smoother.

✦✦✦

Chapter 100 – Conclusion: The Real Science of Manifestation

The Truth

- Manifestation is not magic.
- It is psychology + neuroscience + habit.
- It works when combined with **clarity, affirmations, visualization, and action.**

Key Takeaways

1. **Thoughts → Focus → Action → Results.**
2. Affirmations and visualization train the subconscious.
3. Consistency matters more than intensity.

4. Action is non-negotiable.
5. Living aligned creates long-term transformation.

✦✦✦

Final Message to Readers

Manifestation is not about waiting for miracles. It's about becoming the kind of person who naturally attracts success, love, health, and growth.

When your mind and actions move in the same direction, results eventually follow.

👉 Don't treat manifestation as a one-time trick. Make it your lifestyle.

👉 Start small, stay consistent, and watch your life shift.

✦✦✦

Closing Words

The world is full of hype around manifestation. Some call it magic. Some call it nonsense. The truth lies in between:

- Manifestation is not magic.
- But it is not fake either.
- It is **a mental training system** that, when paired with habits and action, transforms your life.

If you use it the right way — not as wishful thinking, but as a tool for focus, confidence, and persistence — you'll see results in career, health, relationships, and money.

So the final advice:

👉 Don't just wish. Don't just wait.

👉 Train your mind. Take action. And yes — stay consistent.

That is the **real science of manifestation.**

✦✦✦

www.ingramcontent.com/pod-product-compliance
Lightning Source LLC
Chambersburg PA
CBHW022141160726
48282CB00024B/156
* 9 7 8 9 3 3 4 3 9 7 1 1 6 *